AUSTRALIA'S
WILDLIFE

Death Adder

Contents

Common Brushtails are the most familiar of all possums, even in the heart of Sydney and Melbourne. Active at night, they spend the day in dens usually built in tree cavities.

A relative of the domestic dog, the Dingo was introduced to Australia by the continent's earliest inhabitants.

INTRODUCTION

Australia is the lowest, flattest, and driest of all the continents, and its climate the most unpredictable. Most of the interior of the continent is arid with several broad deserts. Only in the south-western and south-eastern corners are extensive wetland and dense forests truly widespread features. The most conspicuous geographical feature is an ancient mountain chain extending from western Victoria up the eastern coast of the continent to the tip of Cape York, known as the Great Dividing Range. These mountains rise to peaks in the Australian Alps, reaching 2228m (7310ft) at Mount Kosciusko (Australia's highest mountain), and in the north at Bellenden Ker, Bartle Frere and Thornton Peak. On the northern slopes, the associated Atherton Tableland, and along the nearby coastline between Townsville and Cooktown some of the world's most important stretches of tropical rainforest occur.

The Australian continent has remained essentially unconnected to other major landmasses since it broke away from the ancient supercontinent of Gondwana some 50 million years ago and began its long, slow drift northward.

Because New Guinea was still connected to the Australian continent for some time after the breakaway, the wildlife links between Australia and New Guinea are very close, whereas those between Australia and other parts of the world are very distant. All these geographical and geological features have had far-reaching implications for the natural history of Australia.

The Green Tree Frog is the largest and most widespread of some 200 species of Australian frog. Its toes and finger discs are large and the upper parts are bright green.

Australian mammals are dominated by marsupials (who give birth to underdeveloped young and usually raise them in a pouch) and monotremes (egg-laying mammals). According to fossil records, these were the only mammal types on the continent when Gondwana fragmented. Though marsupials occur also in North and South America, such characteristic groups as kangaroos, koalas, numbats, wombats and quolls are exclusively Australasian. The continent's wildlife has expanded within the past million years or so because cosmopolitan groups like bats, rats and mice have migrated to these shores. Similarly, Australian birds belong either to very ancient groups, such as emus and lyrebirds, or to cosmopolitan groups that have invaded in the relatively recent past, such as pipits and sunbirds. On the other hand, many groups widespread elsewhere in the world, such as crows and jays, can trace their ancestry to groups that are fundamentally Australian; they have spread outwards from the continent. Two bird families that are especially conspicuous in most habitats, the honeyeaters and the parrots, have radiated in a fashion that to some extent mimics the marsupials; this has resulted in an extraordinary diversity of plumage, structure and lifestyle. Much the same might be said of Australian reptiles and amphibians; most frogs, for example, belong in two families that are exclusively Australasian.

Australia's wildlife is vulnerable to the same varied threats that apply elsewhere in the world. Two of these threats probably eclipse all others, however: land degradation and the impact of feral animals. Soil erosion, inappropriate burning practices, clear-felling, salination, wetland siltation and other abuses have had far-reaching effects that defy assessment, let alone control. On top of this, vital habitats have been severely damaged by the introduced rabbit, as well as by goats, pigs and buffalo, and wildlife numbers have been reduced by predation from feral domestic dogs and cats. The overall impact on Australia's hosts of small reptiles is still being reckoned, but it is known to have been devastating to its populations of small mammals.

Much is being done to prevent further devastations as more and more people come to understand the delicate balance between nature and man; and with such understanding we grow to appreciate and enjoy the unique and special qualities of Australia's wildlife.

Like many other possums, the Common Ringtail (below) often carries its young on its back when they become too big to squeeze into her pouch. The Sulphur-crested Cockatoo (right) requires large tree cavities in which to nest.

MAMMALS

The world's mammals fall into three major groups, and Australia and New Guinea are notable for being the only places where all three occur. The platypus (unique to Australia) and the short-beaked echidna (also found in New Guinea along with the long-beaked echidna) make up the **monotremes**, mammals that lay eggs. Monotremes are unique to this region. **Marsupials** form the second group. They have a furry pouch on the abdomen in which the young are carried. Born at a very premature stage, the young make their way unaided to the pouch where they lock onto one of the mother's teats and continue their development here. In numbers and diversity, Australia is very much the world's marsupial headquarters with kangaroos, wallabies, possums, quolls, koalas and wombats among others. The third major group consists of the **placentals**, the largest, most widespread and most familiar of mammals. Placentals are characterised by the pivotal role of the placenta in reproduction, enabling the embryo to develop to a relatively advanced state within the safety of the mother's womb. Placentals constitute all the familiar mammals – dogs, cats, horses, cows, and also humans. Australia's wild placentals (mostly bats, rats and mice) apparently reached the continent by island-hopping across Indonesia within the last few million years or so, but certainly before the arrival of Europeans and domestic animals.

The Koala is certainly the most popular of all of Australia's unique animals and a very effective ambassador.

Koalas only eat certain types of eucalypt leaves and are commonly found in the eastern and south-eastern forests.

Usually only one young Koala is born at a time, but twins are not especially rare. When the youngsters outgrow their mother's pouch, they ride on her back.

Largest of the marsupials, Red Kangaroos are wide-spread across arid parts of Australia. Their water requirements are low because they forage at dawn and dusk when it is cool, and spend the day loafing in the shade.

Red Kangaroos generally live in small family groups, or mobs. They are very well adapted to drought, despite their diet of grass (a fleeting desert resource), and have a range of mechanisms for coping with unpredictable climatic swings. Females, for example, are ready to breed any time conditions are suitable.

Red Kangaroos drink freely wherever water is readily available. Males, as their name suggests, are usually reddish in hue, but females are often bluish-grey.

The Eastern Grey Kangaroo is herbivorous and prefers somewhat lusher, less arid regions than the Red Kangaroo. It is common in pastoral country across most of the east and south.

Big old males (left) are not much smaller than Red Kangaroos and prefer to live alone. Females look similar, but are smaller and tend to live together in loose mobs. Youngsters (opposite) remain with their mothers even after they are weaned at around fifty weeks of age.

Eastern Grey Kangaroos have a woolly, silvery-grey coat (distinct from the Western Grey which is greyish-brown to chocolate in colour). Like Red Kangaroos, they feed mainly on grass and are strongly adapted to drought. Both are most active at dawn and dusk, resting up in deep shade during the heat of the day.

The Tammar Wallaby (above) is restricted to parts of
southern Australia and a few offshore islands along the coast,
including Kangaroo Island. It differs strikingly from most other
kangaroos and wallabies in that it has regular breeding seasons
and the ability to survive indefinitely on sea water. It is slender,
bare-snouted and has a grizzled, grey-brown coat.

The Common Wallaroo occurs in two populations so
distinct that they have different vernacular names: the Euro
(above) and Wallaroo (right). The Euro is restricted to arid
regions while the Wallaroo inhabits the humid eastern woodlands.
Common Wallaroos live in small groups and graze at night.

Marsupials are notable for their extraordinary diversity of form. Typical among the smaller forms is the Northern Brown Bandicoot (left), a common ground forager of northern and eastern Australia. Marsupials even have carnivorous members, such as the Tasmanian Devil (opposite). Though now confined to Tasmania, it was once widespread on the mainland.

The Platypus (left) and the Echidna (below) are monotremes (egg-laying mammals). Strongly aquatic, the bizarre Platypus was dismissed as a hoax when the first specimens reached Europe in the early nineteenth century. Its features include a soft, rubbery, duck-like bill and a poisonous spur on each hind limb.

The Echidna is widespread across the continent and common in almost all habitats, from the Australian Alps to the interior deserts. It is covered with long spines and has a tubular snout and long mobile tongue. It feeds on many insects, primarily termites and ants.

The Dingo is a descendant of the Indian Wolf and was introduced to Australia somewhere around 35 000 to 40 000 years ago.

Highly valued by the Aborigines as a hunting dog, Dingoes are versatile predators. They have spread across the continent, and occur in packs or as lone wanderers in a range of habitats, from deserts to coastal forests.

A typical Dingo is sandy or gingery in colour, with pricked ears and a bushy tail. It suffers from increasing hybridisation with feral domestic dogs, and in some areas few individuals have an entirely pure bloodline.

BIRDS

There are about 750 species of birds in Australia. The parrots and honeyeaters make up two of the largest and most widespread groups. Pigeons, ducks and several other widely known families are also well represented. Australia has a number of genera that are unique or nearly so. These include lyrebirds, scrub birds, logrunners, currawongs and fairy-wrens. Apart from its resident species, the continent is also the southern terminus of one of the most important bird migration routes in the world. Huge numbers of shorebirds annually arrive on Australian coasts from their nesting grounds on the shores of the Arctic Ocean and elsewhere in the Northern Hemisphere. Similarly, oceanic birds of many species congregate in southern Australian waters in winter.

Australia is the headquarters for some bird families that display remarkable forms of behaviour. These include the mound-builders, or megapodes, who do not incubate their eggs, and the bowerbirds, a family in which the males build sophisticated and lavishly decorated structures of sticks and twigs for the sole purpose of enticing females to mate. Some species even paint their bowers with plant juices applied with a wad of fibre held in the bill. Australia also seems to have far more than its fair share of communally nesting birds – species that form groups, rather than simple pairs, for rearing their young.

The Emu lives right across the continent in a variety of habitats. The largest of the native birds, it stands up to 2m (6.5ft) high and can weigh 50kg (110lb).

*Australian wetlands abound
with wildfowl of various kinds.
The Australian Wood Duck (left)
is perhaps the best known in rural
areas because of its fondness for
stock dams. In northern and eastern
Australia, the Plumed Whistling
Duck (below) is abundant on
permanent coastal wetlands.*

*Huge flocks of Magpie Geese, a bird spectacle of the Northern
Territory, are an image without which no Top End safari
would be truly complete.*

The largest of all kingfishers,
the Laughing Kookaburra is widespread
in eastern Australia, and a frequent visitor to
many a suburban garden feeder.

Kookaburras live in tight-knit communities that cooperate
to raise broods of young together. All group members take
it in turn to incubate the eggs and feed the young of a sin-
gle dominant pair. Kookaburras are most widely known for
their choruses of loud rollicking laughter as the group congregates at dawn and dusk to reinforce the clan boundaries.

*Abundant and widespread throughout the continent, the Galah (opposite),
resplendent in pink and soft grey, ranks among the most attractive of Australian
cockatoos. For many people, a flock wheeling over a paddock (above) is one
of the most strongly evocative images of rural Australia.*

*The Cockatiel is the smallest of the cockatoo family and is easily identified by the bold
white patches on its dark grey wings. It is also one of the few species in which males differ
obviously from females. Males have a bright yellow forehead, face and crest.*

*Like all cockatoos, Little Corellas
need frequent access to water. They
group in enormous flocks.*

25

The Budgerigar vies with the Canary as the world's most popular pet bird. In the wild its natural colour is green and yellow. Its strongly gregarious nature is perhaps its most obvious characteristic.

Australia has been widely billed as the Land of Parrots. When a land bird attracts the attention of a casual observer, it is likely to be a parrot of some kind. Especially conspicuous in coastal forests are rosellas, such as the Crimson Rosella (opposite). The Ringnecks (above) tend to inhabit the arid interior.

Most parrots nest in cavities in dead trees or stumps, like this pair of Blue-winged Parrots. Quiet, elegant, and unspectacular, Blue-winged Parrots are confined to sparsely wooded country in the southern parts of Australia.

Both the Mallee Fowl (below) *and the Scrub Turkey* (bottom) *are megapodes, a group characterised by their breeding strategy. They do not incubate their eggs; instead they bury them in mounds of earth and leaf litter and let solar radiation or the heat of plant fermentation do the job for them.*

Among the most widespread of Australian nocturnal birds, the Tawny Frogmouth (opposite) *is common even in suburban parks and gardens. By day it sleeps on a branch in a distinctive, rigid, upright pose with its bill pointed stiffly upwards, looking very much like a stub of dead wood.*

Bowerbirds reach their greatest diversity in the rainforests of New Guinea, but some occur in Australia. Two species, the Spotted Bowerbird (left) and the Great Bowerbird (top), are common even in arid regions. Male bowerbirds build intricate nests known as bowers (centre) to which they entice females to mate (above). The female then flies off to rear her brood alone.

31

Flamboyant in appearance and behaviour, the Regent Honeyeater (top) is one of Australia's most critically endangered birds. The total population is possibly well below 1000. In contrast, the Noisy Miner (above) is expanding its population in the east and is abundant in the suburbs of many coastal cities.

Honeyeaters are one of the dominant families of birds in Australia, with approximately 70 species. They are common in almost all habitats, including coastal heaths where the New Holland Honeyeater (left) resides. The Macleay's Honeyeater (right) can be found in the tropical rainforests, woodlands and mangroves of the far north.

The Long-tailed Finch is a ubiquitous small bird in the savannah grasslands of the Top End. It lives in flocks and forages the open ground.

The closely related Gouldian Finch is endangered. As for all grassfinches, a diet of dry grass seeds means a constant need to drink, so the birds frequently visit any available source of water.

The Gouldian Finch has notably three forms, or morphs. There is a yellow-headed variety, which is very rare, and a black-headed variety which outnumbers the red-headed birds by about ten to one.

Familiar with cage-bird fanciers around the world, the little Zebra Finch is by far the most numerous and widespread of all Australian grass-finches. The black and white barring on its rump and upper tail gives this finch its name.

Lord of the wetlands and a truly dangerous Australian animal, the Estuarine Crocodile occurs almost everywhere along the tropical northern coasts of Australia.

REPTILES & AMPHIBIANS

Four major groups comprise some 700 species of the reptile fauna of Australia: lizards, snakes, turtles and crocodiles. In some respects this fauna remains little known, and new species are still being discovered and catalogued. Many species, however, are common and familiar to most people. Such conspicuous lizards as shinglebacks and blue-tongues, for example, occur in many suburban parks or gardens, and across much of the arid interior goannas are often the dominant predatory animal. Small reptiles such as skinks and geckos are abundant, both as species and individuals, and most wetlands and waterways support one or more species of turtle. Snakes are common, some are venomous, and a few need to be treated with considerable respect. Fortunately, the number one safety rule for dealing with a venomous snake is easy to remember, simple to perform, and nearly always effective: 'leave it alone'. Much more dangerous is the estuarine crocodile of the tropical coastal waters. A full-grown crocodile is very likely to regard any human in the water as prey. Frogs are most numerous in the east and tropical north, but many species extend across the arid interior as well. Species adapted to arid conditions, such as the remarkable water-holding frog, burrow into the mud and form a sort of water-filled survival chamber of hardened mucus which is bonded to their own shed skin. This allows them to survive for several months or even years of drought conditions.

One characteristic feature of the Estuarine Crocodile is a lower tooth which fits outside the upper jaw (below). It is easily visible even in the newly hatched (opposite).

Easily distinguished by its narrow snout, the Freshwater Crocodile (below) is very much smaller than the Estuarine Crocodile. It does not occur in salt water.

The diet of the Brown Tree Snake (opposite) consists of arboreal birds and mammals such as the bat being disposed of here. Often known as the 'night tiger', it is venomous and will defend itself if provoked but is not generally regarded as particularly dangerous to humans.

The Death Adder is venomous, but only mildly so. The danger lies in the snake's lethargic nature which increases the likelihood of it being accidentally trodden on. Common across most of Australia, it is a 'wait-in-ambush' predator. It lures its 'dinner' within range by the twitching motions of the tip of its tail.

The Yellow-faced Whip Snake may grow up to 1m (40in) in length. Common across much of Australia except the tropical north, it congregates in spring at the same communal mating grounds year after year. It is venomous but not regarded as dangerous.

The Shingleback (above) is a distinctive Australian reptile, instantly recognisable by its stumpy build, short fat tail, broad flat head and the relatively huge knobbly scales from which it gets its name. The Common Blue-tongue (right), despite its much smoother skin, is in fact a close relative of the Shingleback. Both are common and widespread around Australia.

Well camouflaged by its rough warty skin and complex colour pattern, the Southern Leaf-tailed Gecko (below) is nocturnal and hides during the day in cracks and crevices in sandstone boulders and outcrops. It is common, but is restricted to the Hawkesbury sand-stone region surrounding Sydney.

Widespread across northern Australia, the Frilled Lizard favours
open woodland and spends a good deal of its time in trees. Its first
line of defence is to freeze against the bark (opposite), but if hard pressed
it may resort to its famous display (above). Gaping its jaws wide, it spreads
the cape of loose skin surrounding its head in an action reminiscent of
opening an umbrella. It may also hiss loudly and pump its body up and
down, as though hoping to startle its enemy into retreat.

(Previous pages) Bizarre in appearance as well as behaviour, the
Thorny Devil is widespread across the arid heart of Australia. With its tail
curled stiffly over its back, it walks with an odd, jerky, clockwork action. It
feeds entirely on several species of small black ants. It doesn't seek out their
nests; instead it locates their foraging columns on the surface and
gobbles them down as they parade past.

Australia has about 200 species of frogs
and toads, of which many are rare or have
very restricted distributions. In fact a number
of rainforest species of the eastern highlands
appear to have vanished altogether during the
1980s. Others survive but are seriously
endangered, like the green and gold Bell Frog
(left), which is threatened mainly by urban
sprawl and habitat destruction. It inhabits
much of eastern Victoria and New South
Wales, and north as far as Brisbane.

By far the best-known frog in Australia
is the Green Tree Frog (top). This giant –
up to 11cm (4.5in) long – lives in damp
shelters, including man-made cisterns, outdoor
toilets and laundries, from Sydney to Cape
York and westward right across the Top End.
The Eastern Dwarf Tree Frog (above) is
common in open woodland in the east.

47

Australia's only stork, the Jabiru or Black-necked Stork.

First published in 1996
Reprinted 1998
New Holland Publishers Pty Ltd
London • Cape Town • Sydney • Singapore

Produced in Australia by
New Holland Publishers

3/2 Aquatic Drive, Frenchs Forest
NSW 2086, Australia

24 Nutford Place
London W1H 6DQ
United Kingdom

80 McKenzie Street
Cape Town 8001
South Africa

Writer and Photo Researcher: Terence R. Lindsey
Design and Typesetting: Alix Gracie
Publishing Manager: Mariëlle Renssen
Commissioning Editor: Sally Bird
Editors: Thea Grobbelaar, Joanne Holliman
Cartography: John Loubser
Reproduction: Unifoto (Pty) Ltd, Cape Town
Printed and bound in Singapore by Tien Wah Press (Pte) Ltd